MARIE CURIE

by Eve B. Feldman

McGraw-Hill School Division
New York Farmington

Marie Curie, circa 1885

A poor young girl grows up to become so famous that her name is known all over the world. That may sound like a fairy tale, but it is the true story of Marie Curie, one of the most famous scientists of all time. She was the first woman to win a Nobel Prize and the first person to win two of them! The story of her life and of her work is an amazing and dramatic one.

Marie Curie was not born "Marie" or "Curie." Nor was she born rich or lucky or famous. She was born Marya Sklodowska in Warsaw, Poland, on November 7, 1867. She was the daughter of two teachers and the youngest of five children.

Marya was an excellent student despite serious problems at home. When Marya was five, her mother became ill with tuberculosis, a serious lung disease. Marya's mother avoided hugging and kissing her children to keep from spreading her disease.

In 1876, when Marya was nine, one of her older sisters died of typhus, a common disease of the time. Just two years later, Marya's mother died from the tuberculosis she had battled for so long.

Marya's father kept the remaining family together. At night, after the children finished their regular studies, he would teach them more lessons.

At that time, Poland was ruled by its neighbor, Russia. The Russians made a rule that the Poles couldn't teach in their own language. Even so, Marya's father taught his children in their native tongue. He also taught subjects that the Russians had forbidden.

Marya loved learning. She graduated first in her class. She wanted to continue her studies. The Russians, however, did not permit Polish women to go to college.

Marie Curie with her siblings, the Sklodowska children (l. to r.) Zosia, Hela, Marya, Joseph, and Bronya

Marya was determined to learn. How, though, could she learn in a country that would not let her study?

Marie with her father and sisters Bronya and Hela, 1890

Marya studied in a secret school called the "Floating University." Its students met each night in a different location. Marya read books in Polish and learned about other countries where students could study freely.

Marya and her older sister Bronya decided to help each other pursue their studies. Bronya wanted to go to Paris, France, to become a doctor. The sisters agreed that Marya would work to send Bronya to school, and later Bronya would do the same for Marya.

Marya took a job as a governess, a live-in teacher who cared for children. She sent almost all of her money to her sister. In her spare time, Marya gave free lessons to poor village children and read chemistry books.

Marya worked as a governess for three years. Bronya became a doctor and married a doctor. The sisters' plan worked. In 1891, Bronya sent for Marya.

When Marya left for France, she couldn't afford to buy a seat on the train. Instead she carried her own chair. Arriving in Paris, Marya changed her name to its French version, "Marie." Changing her name was the easiest part of her new life. Studying in France was much harder than Marie had expected. French sounded faster and more difficult when spoken by a professor at the Sorbonne, the University of Paris. Marie's lab training was not nearly as good as that of her classmates.

Marie also had a long trip from her sister's house to the university, more than an hour each way in a horse-drawn carriage. That meant that two hours of studying time was lost each day! Marie decided to move closer to the university. She rented a tiny attic room. Often she had barely enough money to buy bread and tea. Sometimes there was not enough money to heat her room. Still Marie was determined to do well.

The Sorbonne, Paris

Marie stayed in the library until it closed at ten o'clock, because the library was heated. Back in her room, she climbed into bed in her coat and continued to study. Her determination was rewarded. In 1893, Marie graduated first in her class in physics. She was awarded a scholarship to continue her studies.

In 1894, Marie received a second degree, in mathematics, and graduated second in her class.

That same year, Marie was introduced to a scientist, Pierre Curie. Pierre and Marie fell in love. Their romance included a shared love of science. Pierre's first gift to Marie was an autographed article about magnetism.

Pierre and Marie Curie in the French countryside, 1896

In July 1895, Marie and Pierre were married. Always practical, Marie decided it would be a waste to buy a white wedding gown. Instead, she bought a dark suit that she could wear to work every day. The Curies took a bicycling trip to the countryside for their honeymoon and then returned to their work, teaching and studying. In 1897, they became parents of a daughter, Irene.

Marie at work with an electroscope

Marie wanted to get a doctoral degree in physics. To get this degree she needed to write a long report, or thesis, on something new. A scientist named Henri Becquerel had discovered that an element called uranium gave off invisible rays. No one had yet studied the rays, however. Marie decided to study this element to find out about its rays.

Becquerel had already shown that the uranium rays caused an electrical charge to build up in the air. Marie decided to measure all kinds of metals and minerals to see if they also caused electrical charges to build up around them. Marie used a machine invented by Pierre Curie and his brother Jacques. This machine, the electroscope, could measure even the tiniest electrical charge in the air. The electroscope would show how strong the rays were by showing how much of an electrical charge they produced in the air.

Pitchblende

Marie measured different rocks. She found one called pitchblende that gave off many more rays than the uranium inside it would have produced. Marie knew that all matter was made up of elements. Marie decided that the extra rays must have come from at least one other element hidden inside this rock.

Marie wanted to find the elements contained in pitchblende, particularly those that were emitting rays like uranium. Marie called these elements "radioactive." She was the first person to use the words "radioactive" and "radiation" for the energy produced.

Marie's enthusiasm for her project was contagious. Soon Pierre decided to abandon his own research on magnetism and join Marie.

The laboratory of Marie and Pierre Curie where the discovery of radium was made

Marie discovered not one, but two new elements in the pitchblende. The first she named "polonium" in honor of her beloved Poland. The second she named "radium," because it gave off rays of energy that spread into the air.

Marie's work was far from easy. The conditions of her laboratory made any research difficult. The lab was a shed, so cold in winter that the temperature went down to about 6° C (about 42° F).

Also, the amount of radium in pitchblende was incredibly small. The Curies had to work through one ton of pitchblende to find one-tenth of a gram of pure radium! The radium, however, was a million times more radioactive than uranium!

The Curies in their lab

Now the two Curies devoted all of their research time to studying radiation. In 1903, Marie received her doctorate in physics. A few months later, the Curies and Henri Becquerel were awarded the highest prize in the world for their work in physics, the Nobel Prize.

Unfortunately, Marie and Pierre were both too weak at the time to travel to Sweden to receive the award in person. They did not yet suspect that the radiation they were studying might be causing them to become ill.

Marie and Pierre Curie shared their knowledge freely. Both decided that becoming rich from their discoveries was against their scientific goals.

Pierre was awarded a teaching post at the Sorbonne with Marie as his lab assistant. Together they tried to avoid the fame that the Nobel Prize brought them. They spent most of their time on their work and with their family. In 1904, their second daughter, Eve, was born.

Then in 1906, tragedy struck. On a rainy day, Pierre Curie stepped into the street and fell in front of a heavy horse-drawn wagon. He was killed instantly.

The Curie Family

Marie with her daughters Eve (left) and Irene

Marie was devastated. She had lost her husband, the father of her two young children, and her science partner. How could she possibly go on alone?

Drawing on the personal strength and determination that had carried her forward all her life, Marie resumed her work. She was asked to take over Pierre's classes at the Sorbonne. She became the first woman in France to become a professor at the Sorbonne. At her first lecture, addressing a packed lecture hall, she began with exactly the last sentence of Pierre's last lecture.

Marie also resumed her research. In 1911, Marie Curie won a second Nobel Prize, this time in chemistry. This second prize recognized Marie's further discoveries about radium. Marie had determined the weight of an atom of radium. Marie Curie was the first person in the world to win a second Nobel Prize.

In 1914, World War I was raging and German bombs fell on Paris. Marie put her one gram of radium, which was smaller than a marble, into a lead box. She took the box into the countryside and locked the radium in a safe deposit box. Then she returned to Paris to take care of the French soldiers.

Marie knew that it was unhealthy to move wounded soldiers. They needed X rays to check their internal wounds. X ray, a form of radiation, produces pictures of the inside of the body. Marie was sure that X rays would save many lives.

She convinced wealthy people to donate their cars and converted these cars into traveling radiology stations. Then Marie learned how to drive, and studied auto mechanics so she could repair the cars.

Taking her seventeen-year-old daughter Irene with her, Marie traveled around in these vans called "little Curies." On the road, Marie changed her own tires and cleaned out carburetors.

Back in Paris, Marie trained hundreds of people as X-ray technicians.

Marie driving mobile X-ray van, 1917

"Little Curies" mobile X-ray vans

Marie did not want to be famous. She just wanted to continue her research. She hated being interviewed. In 1920, however, one American newspaperwoman, Missy Meloney, was very persistent. The reporter finally met and interviewed the famous Madame Curie. The two women became friends. Mrs. Meloney convinced Marie Curie that she could—and should—use her fame to get more radium for her lab. Marie realized that she had to put all her energy into raising money for her lab.

Mrs. Meloney arranged for Marie Curie to visit the United States to meet women who were donating money for a gift of a gram of radium. More than $100,000 was raised! With her daughters Irene and Eve at her side, Marie came to America. So many people wanted to shake Marie's hand that after a few days, her hand had to be put into a sling!

Marie traveled widely. She visited the United States twice and met presidents Warren Harding and Herbert Hoover.

Marie Curie holding a priceless tube of radium presented to her by President Warren G. Harding in Washington, D.C., 1921

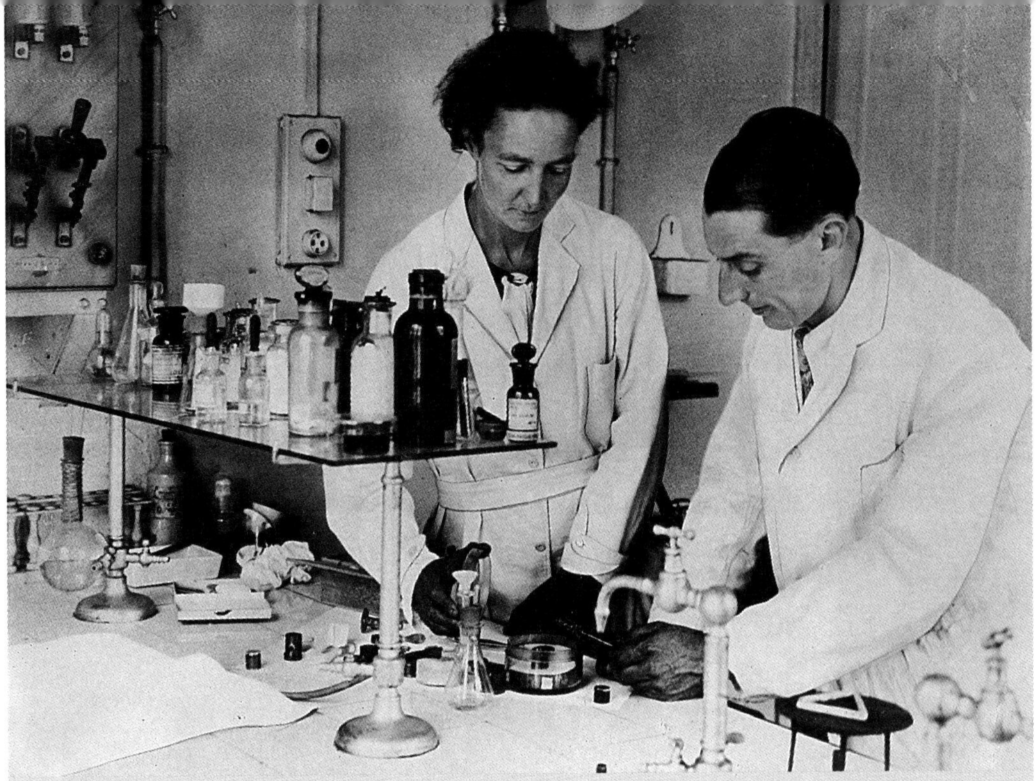

Irene Curie and her husband, Frederic Joliot

Marie was worn out from years of hard work under difficult conditions. Her health was damaged by exposure to radioactivity. No one at that time knew just how dangerous radioactivity could be and how long its effects could last.

Marie's fingers were burned from their exposure to the elements of polonium and radium. Her eyesight was nearly destroyed. Her blood carried the effects of radium poisoning. In July, 1934, at the age of sixty-seven, Marie Curie died from the effects of radium. She didn't live to see her daughter Irene and her son-in-law Frederic Joliot receive the Nobel Prize in 1935 for discovering artificial radioactivity.

It is unlikely that Marie Curie realized just how dangerous radiation could be. Sadly, Irene Curie and her husband Frederic Joliot also died of diseases caused by radiation.

Marie Curie's work led to many advances in scientific knowledge. Radium became a major tool in fighting cancer. Radiation treatments are used today to destroy cancer cells.

Marie Curie

Radioactive dating methods, or carbon dating, can reveal the ages of certain plant and animal remains as old as 50,000 years.

Two major research centers still function as a direct result of Marie Curie's research.

Marie and Pierre Curie were the first to suggest that radioactivity came from changes in the atom. This led other scientists to further research the nature of atoms and how they can be split apart or joined together to release energy. This was the start of nuclear physics. Nuclear physics and nuclear medicine are just two of the new branches of science that can be traced back to the work of Marie Curie. She spent her life and then gave her life trying to uncover some of the mysteries of science. Many mysteries still remain.